Warren Buffett

Invest in the success story of Warren Buffett's life and business as an entrepreneur.

Jason Hamilton

Table of Contents

Introduction.. 5

Chapter 1: The Basics of Warren Buffett............................ 7

    Stock Market 7

    Advice to Others 8

    Growth in Business 8

    Beginning Early.. 9

    Setting Goals... 11

    Staying Humble... 12

Chapter 2: The Earliest Investment.................................. 13

    More into the Business.. 14

    Rules of Investing... 14

    The First Stocks.. 15

    Making More Than His Teachers 16

    Getting Nine Women Pregnant 17

Chapter 3: Passion and Frugality..................................... 19

    Turning Passion to a Career... 19

    The Same House as Always... 21

    Toys are for Children.. 22

    Enjoy Your Life... 22

    Don't Jump on Every Fad 23

Chapter 4: Berkshire Hathaway and Success 25

    A Failing Company... 25

    Warren Buffett to the Rescue....................................... 26

Adding Different Sectors 27

Branching Out..27

The Value of the Company.. 28

Trading... 29

Chapter 5: Warren Buffett's Advice to Owners and Investors.............. 30

On Buying Businesses.. 30

On What Makes a Good Team...31

On Choosing the Quality.. 32

On Business Partners..33

On Conserving Finances 34

Chapter 6: Seeing Success Through Investments 35

Majority of Shares..35

Minority Shares 36

Buffett's Lifestyle 38

Family Time 39

Charity Work... 40

Chasing What You Love... 40

Chapter 7: Quote and Unquote Warren Buffett 42

Inspiring Life 'Quotes' with in depth meaning: 42

Inspiring Business and investing 'Quotes' with in depth meaning:.. 46

Chapter 8: You're Favourite Inspiring Quotes 49

Conclusion.. 50

Introduction

Thank you for taking the time to download this book: *Warren Buffett*.

This book covers the topic of Warren Buffett and will teach you about his life and career. If you want to know the ins and outs of a man that has achieved the highest of heights, then this is the right book for you!

You will find in great depth a great knowledge base of Warren Buffett and how he became the man he is today. Learn how he started out in the early stages of investing with is Dad at the mere age of 11! Warren wasn't always so rich, he didn't inherit the money, he worked smart to give himself the best opportunity he could to achieve this. You don't get to where you want without working smarter and harder than others,

By reading this book you will explore all aspects of the life of Warren Buffett to date and obtain all the knowledge of how Warren achieved what he did. You will find this book to be extremely motivational and inspiring, Warren is quite the intellectual inspiring man that has a lot to give. Motivation and happiness is a huge key to success in Warrens eyes, which is why he does seminars and other events in order to share his knowledge to benefit others and help them get to where he is today.

You will find this book has captured his motivational drive, in addition it includes a whole chapter on motivational Quotes by Warren Buffett himself.

What are you waiting for? Read into the depths of this Informative novella and become more knowledgeable and motived to achieve greater things in life!

At the completion of this book, you will have a good understanding of Warren Buffett and be able to show off your knowledge of him, in acting upon your dreams or simply just taking into consider the mind frame you need to be in to achieve greater things for yourself.

Once again, thanks for downloading this book, I hope you find it to be helpful!

Chapter 1: The Basics of Warren Buffett

Warren Buffett is a businessman who has made a name for himself in the real estate industry. He is an investor and someone who knows how to make money and profit off of things that others may not know about. He has worked hard throughout his life to be able to get to the point he is at, and that has given him the chance to make sure that he is getting everything that he can. He has been investing since he was just a young boy and that has proven to be able to make the success that he has had. He has also been a very humble person throughout that time, and it has allowed him the chance to live the best life he can.

Stock Market

While most people may think of real estate when they think of Warren Buffet, he has actually made a name for himself in the stock market. He has been investing in things that he knew would do well and has shown a talent for choosing the right stocks. This has allowed him the chance to make sure that the stocks that he chooses are profitable and that he is getting the most out of them. It has allowed him the chance to amass his wealth, and it has given him the upper hand on so many competitors who are just able to guess on the stocks. Warren Buffett is almost always able to accurately predict which stocks are going to do well.

All of this has allowed him to remain prominent in the stock market scene. He has always been a major player in the stock market, and he has worked to make sure that he is getting the most out of the things that he is doing. It has given him a chance to do more with his life and with getting the most out of his career. He has been able to do a lot with the stock market, and that is where he has been able to make the most money. He continues to do well and make a lot of money from the stock market and the various investments that he has made with the money that he already has.

Advice to Others

One thing that Warren Buffett has always done is given advice to others. He does not do it in a patronizing manner but does it in a way that shows others he actually wants to help them. He wants everyone to see the same success that he has seen in his lifetime. He knows that people will have a chance to be able to invest in stocks even if that is something that they have never done before. By following the advice that he gives on the stock market, they will be able to get as much out of their investments as possible.

The advice that Warren Buffett gives is valuable and is another way for him to profit off of the things that he has done. He has written books that are filled with advice for people who want to learn from him, he does seminars and talks that allow him to profit and he works to make sure that people are getting his advice. The best part about it is that they are able to get it at not a high cost.

He is a very kind hearted genuine person that if you ever had/could get to know him you should. While Buffett is profiting off of it, the people who are getting it are not paying outrageous amounts to be able to get it – he makes the advice affordable for them.

Growth in Business

The businesses that Warren Buffett has worked with and grown on his own are able to see a lot of growth. They have been successful, and they are all businesses that have good outlooks when it comes to the market and the different things that are going on. This gives people the chance to make sure that they are able to see how Warren Buffett has been successful. There are many different options that come along with these businesses, and Warren Buffett has been able to make good use out of each of them.

The growth that he has created in each of the businesses that he owns and has a part in playing is exponential. He has been able to provide a lot of help to each of these businesses, and the growth has been phenomenal during the time that each of his businesses have been operating. He wants to make sure that they are able to work well with the different options and that they are doing their best to be able to get the most out of the different situations. This has allowed him the chance to make more money while also bringing a high level of success to the businesses that he is a part of.

Beginning Early

Warren Buffett may have very well been born with business in the bloodline but he purchased his first stock at the age of 11. He worked in the family's grocery store in Omaha to help and save a little bit of pocket money. His father, Howard Buffett, owned a small brokerage and when Warren had spare time as a young boy he would go to work with his Dad. At an early age, Warren began leaning what investors were doing and listening to what they said on the phones alongside his Dad.

As a teenager, Warren took on odd jobs, from delivering newspapers, selling coke to washing cars. Using his savings from these he invested in purchasing several pinball machines that he placed in local businesses to profit from.

His entrepreneurial success as a young boy did not immediately translate into everything he desired. His Dad pressed for him to continue his learning after secondary collage, with high reluctance Warren finally agreed to attend the University of Pennsylvania. He then later transferred to the

University of Nebraska, where he achieved a graduate certificate in a three-year business degree.

Once Warren completed this goal in his life he then lead on to set another in wanting to learn more in business, he attempted but failed in applying for Harvard Business School and enrolled in Columbia Business School instead. Just because you fail in getting one thing that you want shouldn't stop you from continuing the pursuit. Warren was taught by Benjamin Graham and David Dodd at this university, both well-known security analysts. Buffett was a huge fan of quite a lot of books but he quite enjoyed Graham's book "The Intelligent Investor". It was under Grahams teaching that Buffett learned the core fundamentals of value investing.

When he graduated from Columbia Buffett intended to work on Wall Street, but with Grahams advice he listened and made a different career choice. In Omaha, Warren worked as a stockbroker and whilst working there opened a number of partnerships. The size of the investing partnerships grew dramatically, and by the time Warren hit the age of 31 he had become a millionaire.

It was at this point here in -1961- that his sights had been turned from simply investing in stocks to investing in business. He made a $1 million investment in a windmill production company, and within the next he made a second in a bottling company. Warren used the value investing techniques he had learnt from graham and found amazing bargains that multiplied his money.

As he was continuing to grow he discovered a textile manufacturing firm named Berkshire Hathaway and began buying shares in that. He made such large amount of investments within this company that he took control of the company in 1965. Like Hathaway, Warren made some other good investments such as American Express, a company that doubled its worth in a matter of two years.

Warren Buffett's investments went always successful and payed off with great dividends, but they were always well thought out and followed value principles. He ensured that, what he was investing in had a certain level of high value and by keeping an eye out for new opportunities, staying true to his morals and strategies it payed off.

Warren Buffett has always been someone who has been successful. He started out with success when he was just in elementary school, and that has continued throughout his life in the investment field. When he was just 16 years old, he was making as much money (if not more than) the teachers who were teaching him to do simple things like math and science. He made sure that he was always working to make more money and that allowed him to have a net worth of over 50,000 dollars by the time that he was old enough to drive.

The early beginning that Warren Buffett had was enough to set him apart from other investors. He took chances, he tried different types of investments, and he made sure that he was always working to be better at the different things that he did in the investment sector. Since he started so young, by the time that he was an adult and others who were the same age were just getting started, he had years of experience behind him and was ready to become an even better investor.

Setting Goals

Ever since he was a child, Warren Buffett had a lot of goals for himself. He knew what he wanted, he kept track of it, and he went after it so that he would be able to reach the goal that he had. This is what made him able to do more with the different options that he had, and it allowed him to always get where he wanted to be in his financial life. He is now worth over 70 billion dollars, and that is because of the goals that he originally set for his financial career.

The goals that he set were not lofty. He wanted to make a few extra dollars and set out to do so. Once he did that, he created a new goal. He was always coming up with new goals and crushing them when he got to the point where he was close to accomplishing them. The goals that he set for himself were sometimes unrealistic, but he was always able to meet them.

Buffett never gave up the goals that he had, and he always persevered toward being better and making more money with what he had available to him.

Staying Humble

Despite the fact that Warren Buffett is one of the richest men in the United States and even around the world, he has always stayed humble. He likes nice things, but he is not flashy with the money that he has. He tries to stay as humble as possible and live as if he were the same person that he was when he first got started with investing in Omaha, Nebraska. He has been able to create a life for himself that is comfortable but is not extravagant, and this has given him the chance to do more with that life.

The humility that he exhibits has been able to show people that you can have a lot of money without becoming ostentatious. This is the way that Warren Buffett has lived his life throughout his time doing business, and it has given him the chance to make sure that he is doing more with different things. There have been many times when Warren Buffett could have flashed his wealth, but he did not and chose to, instead, stay gracious with the money that he has and the opportunities that he created for himself.

Chapter 2: The Earliest Investment

The first investment that Warren Buffett ever made was in Coke. This was something that he liked, and he knew that his friends all liked. For that reason, he wanted to be able to offer it to his friends. This is the way that the investment went:

Buffett and his friends often paid around 10 cents for a bottle of Coke at the grocery that they went to on a regular basis. They did this so that they could enjoy it but they were usually only able to have enough money to buy one bottle at a time. Instead of buying Coke on a regular basis, Buffett sat back and saved up the money that he would have been spending on single bottles of Coke. He had a plan in mind. After he had saved up enough money to buy the Cokes in packs. He saved up one dollar and purchased 4, six packs of Coke (they were 25 cents for a 6 pack) from his grandfather's grocery store. He now had 24 bottles of Coke. He let his friends know that he was selling them for 5 cents a piece (instead of the regular 10 cents that they were used to paying). His friends got a deal, and he was able to make profit a nickel off of each of the 6-packs that he purchased. He profited 20 cents from the first 4 packs that he bought and his friends were hooked – they were getting Coke for half the price that they would normally pay! Instead of spending the money that he made, Buffett would consistently reinvest it back into his Coke business. He would, though, occasionally, gift himself a Coke out of the ones that he bought. It was his favorite drink, after all.

To this day, Warren Buffett still has a fridge stocked with Coke and will almost always order one when he goes out to eat.

More into the Business

Despite the fact that Warren Buffett did like Coke, he knew that he would not be able to grow his business in the way that he wanted if he only had one product. He knew that his friends wanted more than just to be able to get Cokes from him so he chose to invest his money in different products that he would then sell at a profit to his friends. He was like a traveling convenience store, and his friends liked that they were able to get things for cheaper than what they would normally pay at a convenient area because Warren Buffett would travel to them instead of them having to go to the store.

Some of the things that he included in his traveling store were gum, candy, and even magazines. He also peddled magazine subscriptions to his friends so that they would be able to look at the magazines anytime that they wanted. He did this to not only help himself but to also help his friends with the things that they wanted to be able to get each time that they did different things.

It was a good thing that he was doing, and he was actually able to make money. While the rest of his friends were spending every penny that they had on Cokes, candy, and even trading cards, Warren Buffett was squirreling the money away hoping to save up enough to be able to purchase a stock or some other type of investment that would be able to pay off much more than what just selling convenience goods to his friends would. He knew that there was more to investing than just buying at retail and marking up.

Rules of Investing

Since Warren Buffett can definitely be considered an expert on investing, he has come up with two definitive rules that are never to be forgotten when you are investing.

Rule no. 1: Never lose money

Rule no. 2: Never forget rule no.1

These rules apply to any type of investing, and you should take them into account each time that you make an investment. Don't try to go into debt to be able to make an investment – you will almost always end up losing money, and you won't be able to get that money back because of the debt that is going on in your life. You will get behind, and you may not ever be able to get back to where you were at with the money that you had in the beginning. Remember this all of the time that you invest and with everything that you put your money into.

If you are passionate about something and you want to invest in the way that Warren Buffett did, you should save your money and prepare for a long time to be able to make a big investment. This is something that will allow you to have a better chance at making money from the investment and will also give you a chance to not lose money by going into debt.

Even if you have to wait for a long time to be able to save up that money, it will pay off for you. Having some patience will be the best way to prepare for a life of financial stability. It will also allow you to see that waiting can bring about success. Nothing great was created overnight and saving up your money will allow you to be able to have more of it in the long run.

The First Stocks

All of the profits that Warren Buffett was not putting back into his convenience business were going right into savings. He wanted to save as much money as possible so that he would be able to get the things that he wanted later in life. He knew that he could make more money and he had a lot of plans to be able to do it. He saved up a lot of money – more than the average adult during that time made each week – and prepared to be able to buy his first stocks.

The first shares that he ever purchased were with Cities Service Preferred. These were what he saw a lot of value in and knew that they would be stable. He trusted that he would eventually be able to make money off of them and was comfortable with buying three of them at 38 dollars apiece. This was a lot of money, but he had faith that they would pay off. His stockbroker father fully supported his decision to spend nearly 100 dollars (which was worth much more than it is today) on a share. Buffett knew that people would always need the services and that they would be able to stay in business for a long time.

Shortly after Warren Buffett purchased these shares, the price of them dropped down to 27 dollars per share. This was a huge drop and left Buffett slightly panicked that he had made a bad decision. He stayed true, though, and held onto the stocks. They again rose in price and were worth much more than what he had purchased them for. This was the first time that he had bought stocks and the first time that he had seen the rise and fall of the stock market at work. He was hooked and knew that he was going to be able to keep making the same investments in stocks and even businesses.

Making More Than His Teachers

When Warren Buffett was 16 years old, the average teacher at his high school was making around 150 dollars per week. This was a modest amount of a teaching salary but was something that most of them were able to live off of. When Warren Buffett was 16 years old, he was making an average of 175 dollars per week. He made more money per week than the people who were teaching him how to function in the world that he was a part of.

The thing about Buffett, though, was that he was not buying hot rod sports cars or taking girls on expensive dates like the rest of his friends who were making maybe 5 dollars per week working as soda jerks. Even though he was making much more money than these people, he was still living like he was just a poor high school student. He saved money in every way that he could, and the only frivolous spending that he made was in the occasional Coke that he purchased from the grocery store (he just couldn't get enough of that stuff).

While Warren Buffett was working the stock market, he was making a lot of money, and he was saving it up to be able to start his own business. He loved making money from the stocks but decided that the only way that he would be able to make the best investment possible would be to start his own business and invest in himself. The saving habits that he set up during that time would continue throughout his life, and he would eventually become known as the most frugal billionaire in the world.

Getting Nine Women Pregnant

This title may come as a surprise to you considering the squeaky-clean record that is held by Warren Buffett, but this is more of a theoretical thing. One of the virtues that he talks about is:

It takes nine months to make a baby inside of a woman's body. You can't make a baby any quicker if you get nine women pregnant and they are pregnant for one month at a time.

The point of this is that you need to make sure that you are making the *right* investment and that you are waiting the period of time that you need for it to mature. While some investors think that having a huge portfolio filled with ten different types of investments is the way to go, Buffett feels that having one portfolio filled with an extremely high-quality investment is the only way that you will be able to make money from the investment – and he's the one who is worth over 70 billion dollars.

Warren Buffett didn't get nine women pregnant. He simply used it as an analogy to show that you can get more money when you go for higher quality instead of quantity. He also wanted to show that being patient is one of the best ways to make sure that you are making good investments. If he would have gotten rid of the services stock when it plummeted down to 27 dollars per share, he would have lost money from it and would likely not be where he is today. Instead, he held onto it until the price went back up. His patience paid off with those shares.

Chapter 3: Passion and Frugality

Warren Buffett often talks about how it is important to do what you are passionate about. While many people may think that this is not possible because they cannot afford to be passionate, he wants them to know that there are ways to be able to be passionate without spending a lot of money. He is living the dream, and he loves the job that he has. He thinks that you can do the same thing, too. There is so much to be passionate about, and he knows that doing that will allow you the chance to make sure that you are getting the most out of life.

With the advice that he has given, Warren Buffett wants people to know that they can be both passionate and frugal. They can make the money that they want while they are doing things that they love. He wants everyone to know that there *is* more to life than just the 9 to 5 workday and that you can enjoy it if you give yourself the chance to be able to get more out of life. By being both passionate and frugal, you can get exactly what you want out of life.

Turning Passion to a Career

The job that Warren Buffett does is not the most exciting job in the world, but it is something that he loves. He enjoys the stock market, learning the ins and outs of it and beating it on a regular basis. He also enjoys working to make sure that he is making more money and has as much success as possible.

If you do something that you love, you will never have to work a day in your life, and Warren Buffett knows that all too well. He does not consider the work that he does actual work, and it is something that he is confident about. It is also something that he is good at. If Buffett had continued selling Coke and become a retailer, he probably would not have liked his job as much as what he does. If he had gone to Harvard and entered a business career right away, he would probably not have enjoyed his job or been as successful. Instead, he chose something that he was passionate about and figured out how to make it his career.

Since Warren Buffett was passionate about money, growing money and learning how to make money, he knew that is what his career would have to be. He saw it as a way for him to "get better" at life and he turned that into something that he loved each time that he made a new investment. He was great at it, too and ended up being one of the only people to ever beat the market that he was trying to get the most out of. He turned his passion into a career, and he knows that others should be able to do the same – even if they don't have 70 billion dollars saved up. He didn't have that much to start with and simply started saving the little bit of money that he *did* have to be able to invest it later on.

The Same House as Always

Warren Buffett purchased a house in the 1950's and paid just under 35,000 dollars for it. The same house today would have cost him around 260,000 dollars which are a modest amount for a house, especially one that is located just out of a city like Omaha. He got a great deal on the 5-bedroom house, and it was exactly the size that he needed to be able to raise his five children.

The car that Buffett drives is also more suited to a semi-successful small business owner – it is a decade old Cadillac that he purchased for the right price. Before that, he drove a beat up Volkswagen Jetta. He only purchased the Cadillac because of the safety features for his great-grandchildren and because the Jetta had stopped running on him. He has never purchased a brand new car in his life which shows that doing so may be a bad investment. You may want to begin asking yourself what Warren Buffett wouldn't do! He sees that cars lose a lot of value when they are brand new, and he doesn't want to take that kind of risk even though he would be fine to buy hundreds of Cadillacs and not even make a dent in his billion dollar bank account.

He chooses to not spend money on frivolous things. He shops for discount groceries, clips coupons and tries to always get his way to a deal. He saves a lot of money and also donates a lot of the money that he has made.

Everyone has one, though, so what is Warren Buffett's guilty pleasure for spending wasteful money? He buys and drinks around 5 bottles of Coke per day and will spend just about anything on books – he loves a good read.

Toys are for Children

Warren Buffett may have a house that is filled with toys for his grandchildren, but that is the only place that you will find toys in or around his house. He does not purchase yachts, islands in the South Pacific or even second homes that he uses to vacation (he has children he can stay with when he wants to have a vacation). He thinks of expensive toys as just that – another expense that he would have to deal with on a regular basis.

He does not see any value in these things and instead places his value in things that he will get a return from. For example, the one major purchase that he made that most would consider a "toy" is his private jet. He purchased it so that he would be able to save time and money going between different cities. He has to travel a lot, and that is something that he was comfortable with, but he was spending too much money on commercial flights. By making the investment into his own private jet, he is able to save a lot of money.

You won't find bottles of Crystal and high definition televisions on the jet, though. It is a bare bones investment and something that he uses strictly for travel. He does not use it so that he could fly in luxury and would actually prefer flying commercial other than the fact that it would cost him much more money. He has stated that if he *does* have to fly commercial for any reason, he always sits in the economy because it helps him to stay level headed and not become obsessed with the money that he has made.

Enjoy Your Life

Since Warren Buffett has made a career for himself out of living a life that he is passionate about, he knows that there is a lot of value in being able to enjoy yourself. Instead of wasting his money on things like yachts and second homes, he uses his money to buy himself something that he knows that he needs to be able to be happy – freedom. While he was a busy person in his younger days, he always made time to enjoy himself. With the net worth that he had, he was able to pay for people to do things for him and, to him, that is worth so much more than any other type of junk investment that he could have made with it.

The majority of his days are spent reading. He goes to the office, has a few appointments and then puts his nose right back into the book that he was reading. There are many times when he simply chooses not to do a lot of work because it is not something that he does.

Another way in which Buffett enjoys his life is by sipping on Cokes and eating ice cream for breakfast. He is notoriously unhealthy, but that is something that plays into his "life enjoyment" attitude. He does exercise to help keep himself healthy, but he does it only so that he will be able to continue enjoying the unhealthy food that he gorges himself on for as long as possible. He thinks that everyone ought to enjoy their own life in their own way on their own time. Finding a career that you can be passionate about will allow you to have that opportunity.

Don't Jump on Every Fad

As someone who has a lot of money, it would be easy for Warren Buffett to jump into every fad that comes on the market. He could buy the latest tech gear, get the best things possible and try to make things that are different depending on the different attitudes that he has, but he doesn't. He wants only to be able to live a life that is simple and grants him a lot of freedom. He sees fads as something that will come, go and be a waste of money in the meantime.

Warren Buffett only has a flip phone, and he does not keep a computer in his office. He has an encyclopedia that still gets used on a lot of occasions, and he makes sure that he is getting the most information possible out of it. One thing that Warren Buffett does see a lot of value in? The Internet. While it may have started out as just a fad, it is something that he now cannot live without. It makes his business deals much quicker and gives him a chance to save more time. The only problem that he has with it is that he thinks that it is far undervalued for the worth that it has to so many people (including himself).

Chapter 4: Berkshire Hathaway and Success

Even if you have never heard the name Warren Buffett (which most people have), you probably have heard of Berkshire Hathaway. Maybe you have seen the real estate sector of it advertising a home for sale, or maybe you have seen it on the stock market. No matter what, Berkshire Hathaway is synonymous with success and has been a big player in the way that conglomerates are held. It does not have just one goal or purpose but, instead, has many. It is a major player in many different industries including real estate, investing and advising.

A Failing Company

When most people think about Berkshire Hathaway, they associate it with success and with being able to do better from things that are going on, but Berkshire Hathaway was not always successful. When Warren Buffett first became the largest shareholder in the company, it was actually failing. It was just a textile company that was doing poorly when Buffett took it over and made it into what it is today. He didn't turn it into anything that it wasn't before, but he simply made it better than what it was. He expanded on it, and it allowed him the chance to make sure that it was more successful.

The company was about to go under when Warren Buffett came in. This was the first time that he had made such a large investment and what he had been trying to do for his whole life. He wanted to be able to have his own business, and he saw the option of purchasing a failing business the best way to be able to do this. He knew that it was already established and that it would just take some tweaking to be able to get it to the success that he could benefit from and that would be able to keep it in business.

Warren Buffett to the Rescue

Since it is clear that Berkshire Hathaway is still in business today, it is also clear that Warren Buffett did something that makes the company better. He took it from a failing textile company to one of the biggest traded companies in the world. He used both his expertise in the stock market and his business knowledge to be able to get the business back to where it needed to be. He wanted to make sure that it was going to be the most successful business possible and he did not see the option of failure as something that he was willing to deal with.

When it came time for Buffett to make the decision on what he was going to purchase, he chose Berkshire Hathaway for several reasons. He did not want to see the business fail – it was something that he has said of a lot of businesses, he doesn't like to see good businesses go down just because they are not managed the right way. He also thought that having an established business was going to be able to help him make the right choices.

Buffett never thought that Berkshire Hathaway would be what it is today. He had some initial goals for the company and began to reach those goals in just a short period of time. As he accomplished each of those goals, he would set new ones that would allow him the chance to make sure that the company was doing the best possible in the industry that it was making a name for itself in. Warren Buffett was able to rescue Berkshire Hathaway from obscurity and make it one of the most successful businesses in the world.

Adding Different Sectors

The first thing that Buffett did with the company was to add different things to it. He knew that it was going to one day be a conglomerate, but he did not know how big it was going to be. He first added something other than the ability to produce textiles. This allowed it to become a multi functional company and it started to see a lot of improvement in the money that it was making. He also worked to make sure that he was going to be able to have the capital that was required to bring in a lot of money. He did this by adding, even more, sectors to it and making them each successful in their own way.

As the holding conglomerate for each of the smaller companies, Berkshire Hathaway has seen a lot of success and has been able to make more money than some companies that even do the same things. Because Warren Buffett saw that there was a lot of value in the company and in making sure that the company was able to have more parts to it, it was able to be more successful.

By adding different sectors, Warren Buffett set Berkshire Hathaway apart from other companies and allowed it to be as successful as possible. He was also able to go from a simple investing career to having a business that was something that many people invested in. This was always his long-term goal, and it happened in the form of a conglomerate like Berkshire Hathaway that has seen a lot of success.

Branching Out

Warren Buffett knew that his company was not going to be able to go anywhere unless he branched out and made it a publicly traded company. While he continues to be the biggest shareholder in the company and has made himself the essential owner of it because he has so much invested in it, he allows others to make investments into the company. While he has been able to do this, it has also increased the value of the company to a point where he does not need to worry about the different things that are going on with it and with the different options that are included with Berkshire Hathaway.

Since Buffett branched out and opened the company up to different sectors, he was able to make a name for himself and to create more options for the people who wanted to use the holding company to their own benefit. This allowed him the chance to do more with the company and to make more money. It also gave him a chance to see that there was more to trading than just investing in stocks and selling them at a high price. He saw that there were so many benefits to having his own business that he was the majority shareholder of. He knew that the success would eventually lead to him being able to have the financial freedom that he had desired since he was just a young child.

The Value of the Company

Because of the way that the company is set up to be able to umbrella over all of the smaller companies that are included with Berkshire Hathaway, it is able to have a lot of money and be able to increase the value on a regular basis. This has allowed the company to grow not only in physical size but also in the value that it has.

The company that was once failing and was not expected to make it to the next calendar year is now so much more than that. Thanks to the Buffett's expertise and his ability to make things better than what they once were, Berkshire Hathaway is now worth over 200 billion dollars. It is one of the biggest companies in the United States and is second only in value to Microsoft (Similarly, Warren Buffett is second only in net worth to Bill Gates – the creator of Microsoft and a good friend of Warren Buffett).

With the high value that comes along with Berkshire Hathaway, it has given Warren Buffet and the others who are a part of the company the chance to be able to make more money. He has been able to profit from it, and it has allowed him the chance to see what success truly means. Coming from humble beginnings and working hard to invest in different things has paid off for Warren Buffett – one of his goals was to own a successful company and having one with a valuation of over 200 billion dollars. This has brought him quite a far way from making 20 cents off of six packs of Coke.

Trading

The company was created to be traded. It was something that Buffett was comfortable with and confident in his skills of. He wanted to make sure that he had a company that would be able to be traded and that it would allow him the chance to make sure that he was still able to work with the stock market – something that he was passionate about. For that reason, he used Berkshire Hathaway as an "in" into the market and to get his business on the stock market.

Since the company is a conglomerate, all of the smaller companies that fall underneath it are also included in the trades and the stocks that are present with the company. It allows Warren Buffett the chance to make sure that he sees a lot of success and that the company is doing well in each of the things that he has. It has given him a chance to be able to do more and has allowed him the opportunity to get more with the things that he is doing. He has been able to see a lot of success during his time in the business and has been able to get more out of it. Warren Buffett does not directly own all of the businesses that are underneath the umbrella of Berkshire Hathaway but he is able to profit off of them with the money that each of them make.

Chapter 5: Warren Buffett's Advice to Owners and Investors

As we have already figured out, Warren Buffett loves to give advice. He likes to let people know that they can do better. He doesn't do it in a condescending way, but he wants others to be able to benefit from the mistakes that he has made during his life. Because of this, he is always ready to answer questions and to give advice to people who are just getting started in the business world. He wants to make sure that people have the same opportunities, and even better opportunities, than what he was given. He had plenty of advice from his father and people who were also in business at the same time as him, but he hopes that more people will be able to get value out of *his* advice than what he was able to get out of the mistakes that he made.

Warren Buffett only wants people to learn from his mistakes.

On Buying Businesses
Buffett lets on that one of the biggest mistakes he had ever made in his career was actually the thing that propelled his career from only investing small amounts of money and making meager money from the stocks to being a huge corporate conglomerate. He found that the purchase of Berkshire Hathaway was actually a bad decision and something that he is *still* trying to recover from today – when the company is valued at over 200 billion dollars. He knows that his company is worth a lot of money, but he also knows that it could be worth so much more if he had made the right decision and chosen to invest in a business that was slightly better than what he had done with Berkshire Hathaway.

He knows now that it is better to buy a great business that has a fair price instead of buying a fair business that has a good price. You can always try to get the price down or raise more money to be able to purchase it, but it is much harder if you want to try to increase the business that you have. If the business is not a good business, it will be very hard for you to be able to make that business better especially if it is doing poorly.

If Warren Buffett could go back in time to the point in which he became the majority stockholder in the Berkshire Hathaway business, he would not buy into that deal. He says that it was one of his regrets because of all of the work that he had to put into it to get it to the point that it is at today. He would have bought a business that was not failing and just tried, instead, to save up the money that he had to be able to buy a better business.

On What Makes a Good Team

A good team is a key to having a good business, but you need to have a strong business to be able to make the good team able to do what they are doing. Warren Buffett loves analogies, and he often compares employees to jockeys. A good jockey is a good jockey. If you put a good jockey on a horse that is good and runs fast, the jockey's talents will shine through, and they will likely win as a team. If you put a good jockey on a terrible, run down horse, they will both fail. The same applies to employees and businesses. Great employees are not going to be able to use their full talents if they are put in a bad business where a bad situation is. There are many different things that go into the business, but great employees will also be able to do the business that much better.

It is always a good idea to have the best employees possible, but you should also watch out for the health of your business.

Try to keep the business as functional as possible. If you do that and you have good employees, just like a racehorse and a jockey, they will both be able to win in the end.

A great team is comprised of people who are able to work well together, who have talents in different areas and who have a drive to always be able to succeed in everything that they do. It is important to have a team that is not only "good, " but that also works well together and is able to get what they need out of business. This has allowed Berkshire Hathaway to be able to grow into what they are today – great employees and people who are working together toward one common goal.

On Choosing the Quality

Every time that Warren Buffett has the chance to choose, he will always choose something that is of a higher quality than to have more of the same thing that has a higher quantity. He does this because he recognizes that quality will go a very long way but quantity may not. He knows that if you have one good pair of Brooks sneakers, they will cost you a lot more than a pair of store brand sneakers. He also knows that the store brand will last you about three months, but the Brooks will last you about 1 year depending on how much you use them. This is something that he has always believed.

When he was first getting started, he did not have the money to make extremely high-quality investments – hence the purchase of failing Berkshire Hathaway. He also knew that if he bought a few of the lower quality ones, he would be able to stop doing that and begin making the money that he needed to be able to buy the higher quality ones in a lower quantity. This is one of the many ways that he has been able to learn from his mistakes.

By purchasing quality – and sometimes paying a little more – Warren Buffett is exemplifying the best frugal attitude that there is. He looks at the value of things and what they are worth and then assesses them to make sure that they are worth it. He does not like to pay a lot of money for things, so he will sometimes wait until the high-quality items drop in price or there is a sale. He will try to get any deal that he can, but he will not sacrifice the quality of the items.

On Business Partners

When Warren Buffett chooses a business partner, it is always someone who he knows that he can get along with. While he is one of the kindest billionaires in the world, he is known to stop meetings with people simply because he does not get along with them or he feels that their personalities clash in a way that would make them unable to work together successfully. He knows that to have the best business possible, you need to make sure that you are with a business partner who you can get along with.

While there are many people who would say that you should not mix business and friendships, Warren Buffett believes the opposite. He knows that people need to make sure that they can get along with their business partners and he thinks that friendship is the only way that you can do that. He actually suggests becoming friends with people long before you make the decision to go into business together. This is something that he feels strongly about, and he will never work with someone who he can't get along with.

There are many different things that he does in business. He has put down many deals that could have been perfect simply because he cannot get along with the person who wants to become partners with him. These could have been great business deals, but Warren Buffett did not think that they would be a good idea because he did not get along with the person who was running the business. He always wants to make sure that he is able to get what he can out of the businesses and knows that he cannot do it without a person who he gets along with.

On Conserving Finances

Berkshire Hathaway has always had a very conservative outlook when it comes to the way that they handle their finances. They have done this because of the way that they are doing things and because the majority shareholder is so frugal with everything in his life. Many people think that this is a mistake on the part of the company and Buffett himself is not even sure if this is a mistake or not but he wants to keep the company the same way as what it has always been. This has allowed them to flourish throughout the time that they have been in business and it has also allowed them the chance to see that they are doing more with the company.

He knows that keeping the business frugal is one of the only ways that he will be able to continue growing it. As a conglomerate with over 40 companies underneath their grand umbrella, Berkshire Hathaway has got to learn how to save the money that they have and to keep the costs low. It would be nearly impossible to add any other companies to the business because they are already so big so that is the only way that they can both save and increase the money that they have.

Chapter 6: Seeing Success Through Investments

Warren Buffett did not get rich by just sitting back and let his money build up. Now that he has established his conglomerate and everything that goes along with it, he *is* able to sit back and enjoy the profits that he has, but that meant that he had to work hard to be able to get what he wanted. He worked only for his freedom and the ability to enjoy his life even though it wasn't that hard to do business when he was still very active in the company – he loved it, so it didn't really work that he had to do. It was more like a hobby that allowed him to make money. The success that he has seen has come through each of his business ventures – some more personal than others.

Majority of Shares

The Berkshire Hathaway group owns a majority of shares in the following companies among others:

- Geico
- Heinz
- Fruit of the Loom
- Brooks (running shoes)
- Helzberg Diamonds
- Dairy Queen
- Berkshire Hathaway Real Estate (and any other companies associated with that name)
- Justin Brand
- The Pampered Chef
- Russell (sports equipment)
- Benjamin Moore & Co

These are all owned by Berkshire Hathaway conglomeration company, but they are owned by 99% or 100% as the majority share. The bigger name brands are owned at 99% with 1% going to other investors while the rest of the companies are owned 100% by Berkshire Hathaway and Warren Buffett. He has done this so that he is able to get his name on different brands and this has given him the chance to be a big part of the market.

While Warren Buffett eschews having a large number of low-quality businesses and investments, he has nothing against having a high quantity of high-quality businesses, and he is able to do this because of a large amount of money he has made in the time that he has been in business. It has allowed him the chance to make sure that he is getting more money and that he is able to get the most out of the various business.

If you notice the list of companies that Berkshire Hathaway owns, they are all vastly different. This is because Buffett sees that there is value in different industries. By owning businesses that have a lot of different varieties in them, it will not matter if one market fails – he will not be affected because he will be able to just rely on the other companies that are a part of the other markets that he is in.

Minority Shares

Just because Berkshire Hathaway owns a lot of companies doesn't mean that they don't have things invested in other companies. The following companies have Berkshire Hathaway as minority investors. This means that the company is not responsible for owning them, but they do have a stake in them. It can be predicted that should something happen with one of the companies and their major investors, Berkshire Hathaway would jump at the opportunity to be able to own the company. These are all minority investments for Berkshire Hathaway:

- Delta
- NOW (oil and gas)
- Charter Communications
- Costco
- American Express
- Apple
- Coca-Cola
- Kraft
- Mondelez
- American Airlines
- John Deere
- General Motors
- IBM
- Johnson and Johnson
- Mastercard
- Bancorp Bank
- Wells Fargo
- M&T Bank
- Verizon
- Visa
- UPS
- 21st Century Fox
- Wal-mart

Each of these businesses has their own majority stockholders that are not related to Berkshire Hathaway. As it is clear to see, Berkshire Hathaway has their hands in many different pots, and this is not the entire list of businesses that they own stock in. There are many small businesses that are not featured on this list in addition to businesses that were not publicly listed. Berkshire Hathaway has a stake in the three biggest credit cards: Visa, Mastercard, and American Express. The only business that they do not own stock in that offers credit cards, and other financial services are Discover. If given a chance, the company would likely hold stock in Discover, too. It is important to note that most these businesses have Berkshire Hathaway holding anywhere from around .3% of the stock to up to 36% of the stock which is much lower than the majority ownership that they have.

Warren Buffett has personally approved each of the companies that Berkshire Hathaway holds stock in. From the largest deals to the smallest ones that are in the business, Warren Buffett puts his personal advice on it and makes sure that they are making the right investment so that they will be able to make the most amount of money possible.

Buffett's Lifestyle

The lifestyle that Warren Buffett lives is much different from what you would typically expect of a billionaire. It is a frugal one, and something that he knows will be able to save him a lot of money. He does not go on expensive vacations, does not flaunt his money and always makes sure that he is doing his best to be able to help people who need it. He thinks that it is important not to have too many things that are extra in his life because that will cause him to have even more expenses and will take away from the money that he has made. He will just have to spend more money to maintain them.

With all of the ways that Warren Buffett is frugal, he has been able to hold onto a lot of his money. Even if he weren't frugal, he would still have a lot of extra money because of how much he is worth.

Despite the fact that he is worth so much money and has made a lot during his time, he does not think of life any differently than what he did before he was so successful. He still values his time on his own and with the people he loves.

He says the only thing that money has been able to buy him that has been worth anything has been the freedom that he now has to be able to enjoy the people who he holds closest to his heart and in his life. It has allowed him the chance to make sure that he is comfortable in a way that no material possessions can provide.

Family Time

Warren Buffett is a family man. He has a lot of values that are centered around his family, being with them and spending time with them. It has allowed him the time to make sure that he is doing things the right way and that his family is the number one priority in his life. With everything that he has, he still considers his family to be his most valuable prized possession.

He often says that his family was the best investment that he has ever made. While he brushes Berkshire Hathaway off like a bad business deal, he constantly raves about his family and how much they mean to him. He knows that, without them, he would not be anywhere near what he is today and that is something that money cannot buy.

Buffett suggests that you treat your family just like a business. Even though it is important to connect with family on a personal level, you should make sure that you are getting the most out of the family life and that you are investing time, energy and (sometimes) a little money into it. There are many valuable things that come from having a great family life, and none of these will even be anywhere comparable to a good business. Your family should be your number one business and it should be the thing is the most important to you in your life. If you do not put your family first, nothing else will come into place, and you will not be able to get the help that you need in your life.

Charity Work

When you have so much money that you don't know what to do with it, you will eventually need to start donating it and find causes that you are passionate about. These can be anything from charity things to everything else that is in between, and it is important to make sure that you are able to get the most out of the charities that you work with. Warren Buffett knows a lot about charity and has donated a huge portion of his billions of dollars to charities that have been able to use the money to make things better for the people that they serve.

Warren Buffet is very close and friendly with the number one richest man in the United States. Buffett and Gates get along with each other. This is, perhaps, because they both have chosen to live lives that are not quite the billionaire outlook (although Bill Gates isn't quite as frugal as Warren Buffett). They get along, enjoy meetings with each other and they even do a small amount of business together. Berkshire Hathaway is a very small stakeholder in Microsoft (as well as Apple – they have the game *down*).

One of the charities that Warren Buffett often donates to is the Gates charity. He also uses his money for other things that he is passionate about. While he has endorsed candidates in politicians, he tries to leave some of the money aspects out of it. He is a Democrat and mostly supports Democrats when it comes to national elections, but he has been known to support some smaller position Republicans – especially those who are running in Nebraska and have agendas that are similar to what he believes in.

Chasing What You Love

The number one reason that Warren Buffett says that he is so successful is that he has always chased what he loved. He loved money but not in a greedy way. It is a challenge for him that he enjoys doing and something that he is comfortable with. Making money *from* money is what Warren Buffett loves to do, and he wants other people to be able to make money, too. This is what he is passionate about.

The passion that he has for money has allowed him to make a lot of it. He is in the business of money, and he knows that it is important to always do what he can to make more of it. Not because he is a greedy person but because he likes learning how to make money from the money that he has. It has given him the chance to see that he can do much more in life and that he can crush goals. This has allowed him the opportunity to do more and to learn more about his own life. It has also given him the chance to be able to help other people with their lives in the process.

Warren Buffett does not do much work now that his company is able to essentially run itself with the great employees that he has. He admits that he spends around 80% of his time reading books and that when he is not doing that, he is most likely doing something that is leisurely to him. He only works about 1% of the time, and even when he does work, it is something that he does not necessarily consider work. He believes that he has never truly worked for a single day in his life because he has always done what he loved and that has made life seem like it isn't just about clocking in and getting a paycheck.

He and his 74-billion-dollar net worth may be onto something here.

Chapter 7: Quote and Unquote Warren Buffett

You will find the most inspiring quotes that have been spoken or written by Warren Buffet within this chapter. The Quotes in which are featured here are carefully selected meaningful one's to motivate and inspire you to reach your full potential in becoming the best you can be!

I believe that you will find them to be both insightful and meaningful, as they are not just a quote. I have carefully gone through them each individually to ensure you understand the true meaning behind them all. You may thoroughly enjoy these quotes and have them pinned up on your wall to fill your mind with positive inspirational words. Use this as your drive to strive!

By simply reading a quote or two a day may be just what you need to ignite the passion and desire for success. However, keep in mind that motivation is worthless unless you act upon what you are trying to become motivated towards!

Take your time read them thoroughly and allow your mind to absorb every bit of wise wisdom from the man himself Warren Buffet.

Inspiring Life 'Quotes' with in depth meaning:

"Someone is sitting in the shade today because someone planted a tree a long time ago."

This quote is meaning that Warren Buffett had done the work earlier in his life to allow him to rest in the shade today. (Not having to work to make money today). The lesson here is to work harder/ smarter while your young and you will have nothing but paradise when your older.

"Chains of habit are too light to be felt but can become too heavy to be broken"

If you wish to know the meaning of this continue reading here...

You will find that habits become passive in life and it doesn't take much effort to do these specific things in life. But if you keep bad habits within your life style for too long, then you will not have the mental or physical strength to break those habits. The lesson here is to break a bad habit early while it is still light, DON'T WAIT until it becomes too hard to break.

"Basically, when you get to my age, you'll really measure your success in life by how many of the people you want to have love you, actually do love you."

The meaning behind this quote is that money is not always success. You can find other measurements of success and one of them being love/friendships. When you grow old you really question how many people you love truly love you as a friend, Dad, Uncle, Grandpa... So, don't be so obsessed with money and take time for those who you love to ensure they love you back.

"Of the billionaires I have known, money just brings out the basic traits in them. If they were jerks before they had money, they are simply jerks with a billion dollars."

This is a brutally true quote, you are who you are no matter the money status. The lesson to take away from this quote is that it doesn't matter how much money you have in life people will see you for who you truly are. If you want people to see you as a good person don't allow money to put your true self in the shade and become a jerk because of money. If you're a good person make sure you stay a good person to other people, no matter how much money you have by showing love or respect to everyone.

<u>"Only when the tide goes out you discover who has been swimming naked."</u>

This is a good quote, I quite like this one. It has the potential for many meanings but I found it to mean when you are going about day to day life in the middle of the day everyone has their business cloths on whether it be the tradesman or the office worker. But when it comes to that time of the day where you take those cloths off you see a person's true colors. It makes you think what do I want people to see when I show my true self.

<u>"Honesty is a very expensive gift. Don't expect it from cheap people."</u>

Honesty is hard to come by sometimes, you can act on this quote by treasuring those that are loyal and honest to you. Another point Warren is saying is you don't want to be expecting people in life to tell you the truth if they are a bad person. You may find yourself constantly mislead if you constantly believe bad people. (Learn to judge who is a good person)

<u>"I don't look to jump over seven-foot bars, I look around for the one-foot bars that I can step over."</u>

You would want to keep in mind that you don't need to set goals that are too high. You need to set realistic one-foot goals that you can achieve with reasonable effort. Because by achieving a large number of small goals, in the end lead to that big seven-foot goal that you tried and failed to achieve at the beginning.

"The most important investment you can make is in yourself."

This quote means exactly that, you need to invest time and money in yourself because you're the one that will make the money. Trust in your own ability, have no doubts and make sure you are always happy in what you're doing. Happiness is the key to a good life because without happiness you will fail in everything. Ensure you do everything to lead you to happiness. Yes, there may be a few steps along the way that you don't like as much but make sure that by doing these steps it will in the end lead you to happiness.

"Opportunities come infrequently. When It rains gold, put out the bucket, not the thimble."

The quote here means that you need to take all good opportunity's in life with both hands not just one hand (don't take opportunity's halfhearted). If you see an opportunity that may lead to a really good thing, then don't hesitate put your mind and body forward to see where it goes. People only come across one really good opportunity occasionally so don't be scared. Whether it be an opportunity to be with a special girl or guy. Or it's an offer to do something nice for someone it can always lead to a bigger and better bucket of gold.

"The best thing I did was to choose the right heroes."

In life, we need to pick heroes or people that we look up to, that will make us achieve the best within ourselves. Warren chose correctly and so can you! Decide on what makes you happy or someone you want to be just like. Then idolize them and push yourself to get to where they are and you will find happiness.

Inspiring Business and investing 'Quotes' with in depth meaning:

"In the business world, the review mirror is always cleaner than the windshield."

The meaning of this quote is that you will find the past is always clearer than the future because it is behind you and you can see what has already happened as opposed to the unknown of what is about to happen.

"If past history was all there was to the game, the richest people would be librarians"

The wording is purposely hard to read to make you read this quote several times in order to really get it stuck in your mind that if you only needed knowledge then everyone who wanted to be rich would become a librarian to obtain this knowledge. In other words, to be successful/rich in this day and age you need more than just knowledge you need to be skillful. You need to not only learn how to play the game, you need to have the skills in order to beat everyone in that game.

"Rule number 1 never lose money. Rule number 2 never forget rule number 1."

In order to know the true meaning of this you need to ensure whenever investing money into something you always obtain the correct knowledge so you can't lose. Research your investment inside and out to find all the potential downfalls and make sure you don't do the same mistake as others do.

"I always knew I was going to be rich. I don't think I ever doubted it for a minute."

The meaning behind this quote is that Warren was always confident in himself and he always made sure that if he lost money it wasn't going to bring him down he would learn from it and turn it around from a negative to a positive.

"The smarter the journalists are, the better off society is. For to a degree, people read the press to inform themselves – and the better the teacher, the better the student."

This particular quote is saying that if you have a smarter teacher then you yourself will become a smarter student. Which is giving you the lesson of, find yourself the best teacher and you will be able to learn better than anyone else.

"It's far better to buy a wonderful company at a fair price than a fair company at a wonderful price."

Initially this quote is directed at saying if you buy a good company at a reasonable price you will be a lot better off than if you were to buy bad company at a cheap price. But in saying that this quote can be directed at a lot more than just a company. It can be used as a prime example for quality over quantity and be used in every business sense. When purchasing or investing in anything in life people much prefer quality over quantity, so ensure you are providing good quality at all times and you will make more money.

"It takes 20 years to build a reputation and 5 years to ruin it. If you think about that, you'll do things differently."

This quote is suggesting that Warren has learnt that it only takes ¼ of the time to ruin a good business. The lesson is to make sure when you are operating a business that one of your main objectives is to maintain or improve the reputation of that business, not destroy it.

"Predicting rain doesn't count. Building arks does."

Here is a clear example of telling you not to sit back and estimate what will happen. What Warren is saying is that you need to act and build something substantial to hold your life together rather than just guess or say something will happen.

"Risk comes from not knowing what you're doing."

In a business sense the lack of knowledge about a specific topic or field that you are investing time and money into is a big risk. Warren Buffet believed if you were going to spend your time and money into something don't make it a risk by not doing all the appropriate research. Make it a sure thing with a few potential bumps on the road.

"It's better to hang out with people better than you. Pick out associates whose behavior is better than yours and you'll drift in that direction."

This quote is quite a judgmental quote but can prove to be harshly true (sometimes). Warren is saying that if you pick friends that have or want to achieve more in life you will find you get pushed and motivated in that direction too. It can be a looked at as a positive statement because if you want more in life then you don't want to be hanging around the wrong people (people that have no care and smoke/drink all day). You want to find people that are successful both in their work and life, you want friends that are happy in life and strive to be better.

Chapter 8: You're Favourite Inspiring Quotes

Which quotes made the top 10 Cut:

1. _____

2. _____

3. _____

4. _____

5. _____

6. _____

7. _____

8. _____

9. _____

10. _____

Conclusion

Thanks again for taking the time to download this book!

You should now have a good understanding of Warren Buffett's business sense and the way in which he views life. You will be able to let others know what you know about him, but not only this you can also act upon these principles yourself!

Don't let the end of this book or something else in life stop you from changing your outlook of life today.

Just take those baby steps toward saving and investing your money into something that will be beneficial. It doesn't matter what you decide to invest your money in, if you make sure you do the correct research and know that the option you choose will be beneficial then that's all that matters. I strongly suggest not investing without all the knowledge in what you are doing because this will not make you the money in the long term.

If you enjoyed this book, please take the time to leave me a review on Amazon. I appreciate your honest feedback, and it really helps me to continue producing high-quality books.

Simply CLICK HERE to leave a review, or click on the link: